MINISTER'S
MARRIAGE MANUAL

Compiled by

SAMUEL WARD HUTTON

BAKER BOOK HOUSE
Grand Rapids, Michigan

Library of Congress Catalog Card Number: 67-18181

ISBN: 0-8010-4031-0

First printing, May 1968
Second printing, January 1970
Third printing, October 1971
Fourth printing, January 1974
Fifth printing, November 1975
Sixth printing, April 1977
Seventh printing, September 1978
Eighth printing, April 1980
Ninth printing, August 1981

PHOTOLITHOPRINTED BY CUSHING - MALLOY, INC.
ANN ARBOR, MICHIGAN, UNITED STATES OF AMERICA

CONTENTS

Part I. CHRISTIAN MARRIAGE

Part II. SOURCE MATERIALS FOR MARRIAGE
(Various Marriage Ceremonies)

PREFACE

The purpose of this small volume is to provide a helpful and stimulating source book relating to marriage. "The Home is God's First and Holiest School," is a familiar motto gleaned from Sunday School conventions of years ago. Its fundamental truth still holds. How important it is, therefore, that the homes of today and the years ahead be fortified through premarital education and counseling, an enriched marriage ceremony and a continuing ministry of guidance in the highest principles of morality and understanding.

In addition to the customary marriage ceremonies, spanning the spectrum from freedom of wording to the closely drawn lines found in the Prayer Book, a new feature has been added to the contents of this manual, viz., Jewish and Roman Catholic marriage services are included by permission.

It is interesting to note that all marriage ceremonies follow a similar path of procedure. In churches where the minister is free to change and enrich the wording, he often will do so to make the service more personal. There is a growing trend toward making the solemnizing of marriage a deeper, more meaningful experience.

Suggestions are included in this book to assist the clergy in education, premarital counseling and guidance. A list of suitable music, both instrumental and vocal, is included along with a classified list of appropriate books for reading. It seems unnecessary to give detailed state laws relating to marriage and divorce, but a summarizing table included herein may be helpful. Particular emphasis is given to a continuing ministry to the couples a minister marries. This seems to be good strategy. Every minister will develop his own procedures. This book may help. Use it not as a crutch but to stimulate initiative.

S. W. Hutton

PART I

CHRISTIAN MARRIAGE

Premarital Counseling

Processional and Recessional Diagrams

Wedding Etiquette

The Ring in the Wedding Ceremony

Music for Church Wedding Ceremonies

A Continuing Home Ministry

A Home Dedication Service

A List of Marriage Anniversaries and Appropriate
Gift Suggestions

A Table of Marriage Laws

Grounds for Divorce

A Scriptural Marriage Ceremony

A Brief Marriage Ceremony

A Marriage Ceremony Included within a Complete
Order of Worship

A Communion Service to Be Included in the Marriage Service

Chapter 1

PREMARITAL COUNSELING

Premarital counseling widens into a planned program of education, guidance and counseling. Significant strides are being taken today toward helping those contemplating marriage within a month, two months or after a longer period of time. In fact the churches are beginning to see the total related field of education, guidance and counseling. Classes are being set up in the church school, community wide training schools, and in our colleges and universities to strengthen the home life of our country. We are dealing with life at its source, and seeking to build the foundations of physical, mental, social and spiritual life that the level of character development may be lifted. Both church and state have a stake in this enterprise. Home, church, and community are involved.

As a result of purposeful training in college, university and seminary class rooms, ministers are recognizing the great value of premarital interviews. In some marriages the minister has no choice but to act quickly and to depend heavily upon the solemnity of the marriage ceremony itself; but where it is at all possible for him to interview both the man and the woman separately, he may do so with effectiveness. Within a practical frame work of reason and in the spirit of encouragement, he may include in these interviews:

1. *A social approach* —

   How long have you two known each other?
   For what period of time have you been engaged?
   Have either of you been engaged before?
   What interests do you have in common?
   What is your attitude toward your future inlaws?

2. *An economic approach —*

Will both of you work, or only one?

What will the combined income be?

Have you considered working out a budget of expense in keeping with your total income?

Do you plan to rent, or will you attempt to buy a home?

Which of you will control the purse strings?

Is either of you inclined to be extravagant or a "tight wad"?

Do you plan to open one or more charge accounts?

3. *A personal approach —*

State law requires that each of you take a blood test.

It is wise for the woman to have a complete physical examination.

What is your attitude toward children? A practical pamphlet or book may be helpful. (See page 94)

Have you had any arguments?

Do either or both of you have quick tempers?

What recreation can you both enjoy together?

How will you face discouragement or elation?

Are there any particular problems that bother you?

Are you deeply in love with one another?

4. *A spiritual approach —*

What is the church background of each of you?

If you come from different faiths, what are your plans for agreement?

Have you considered asking a blessing on the food before each meal?

What has been your experience and practice in prayer?

Have you carried a responsibility in your local church, such as leading a youth group, teaching in the church school or singing in the choir?

Some have found a brief devotional at the breakfast table helpful. Various booklets are available.

The minister would do well to inquire into the reading

habits of both the man and woman, and point out appropriate books, magazines and booklets.

5. *Preliminaries to the marriage —*

Within the period of premarital counseling, the couple should be made familiar with the ceremony to be used and all the details relating to it so no embarassment may occur to anyone. These matters are covered in detail in the chapter on "Wedding Etiquette."

Sermons, classes, reading, problems both personal and general, are due for consideration.

The structure of premarital interviews would include marriage itself, economic considerations, sex in relation to parenthood, the in-law question, emotions, church affiliation. All these should be dealt with in counseling. The home has primary responsibility at this point to "train up a child in the way he should go."

Not every minister has had adequate training to do thorough counseling and to give guidance. Where possible he may take further training in this art, or call on someone trained in this field to help him. Both time and skill are essential for best results.

6. *The marriage service itself —*

This important matter is considered in the chapter on "Wedding Etiquette," and is inherent in the various ceremonies offered in Part II as samples to guide the minister and all parties concerned.

The details should be talked over by the minister and the contracting parties ahead of time so that all movements and the dramatics so full of meaning and yet simple, may be carried through with dignity, happiness and due solemnity.

Note: Thanks to Dr. Charles F. Kemp, Brite Divinity School, T.C.U. and Charles Sanders, University Christian Church, Fort Worth, Texas, for their expert guidance in this chapter.

CHAPTER 2

PROCESSIONAL AND RECESSIONAL DIAGRAMS

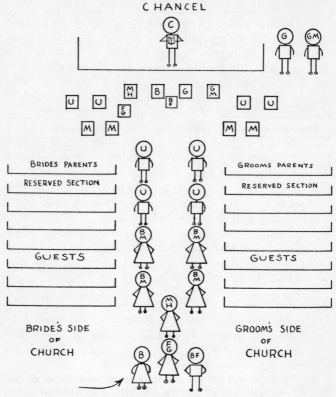

THE PROCESSION

The wedding procession may vary. This diagram suggests four ushers and four bridesmaids, two of each on either side. Note the figures as they enter, then the station for each person.

Meaning of symbols: B - Bride, G - Groom, MH - Maid (or Matron) of Honor, C - Clergyman, GM - Groomsman, BF - Bride's Father, U - Usher, FG - Flower-girl. A ring-bearer may be included if desired

It is understood that the clergyman, the groom and the groomsman will enter from the right side of the chancel when possible. Others will enter from the rear.

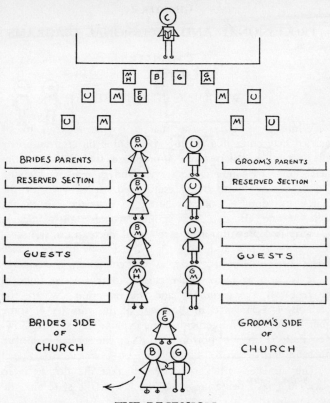

THE RECESSION

Moving from their stations the wedding recession leaves as indicated, the bride and groom leading the way. The bridesmaids may walk side by side, followed by ushers, or walk with ushers. The groomsman will walk with the maid, or matron, of honor. The flower-girl walks immediately behind the bride and groom.

CHAPTER 3

WEDDING ETIQUETTE

While it is quite true that a couple seeking to be married may enter this all-important union on civil authority only, yet it is much more appropriate for the church of their choice to conduct the service and to give its blessing upon the new home being established. It is wise for the church to adopt a policy relating to marriage within the walls of the church. This policy would rightly include planning and preparation, the rehearsal, decorations, the wedding, photographs and fees. A printed copy of the policy should be available for couples contemplating marriage.

It is wise to keep rather closely to traditional lines in the rehearsal, the ceremony and the reception. Where the ceremony is performed in the home of the minister or some other home, the arrangements are comparatively simple; however, there is every opportunity to make the service beautiful, inspiring and deeply religious.

The minister will satisfy himself that the license is in order. Marriage brings together the law of the state and the sanction of the church.

In further detail it would be well to follow this procedure —

I. Planning and Preparation
1. Make an appointment with the minister of the church where the ceremony will be performed.
2. Select the minister to preside at the wedding.
3. Arrange for a period of counseling in line with the desire of the minister.
4. Make reservation for both the rehearsal and the

wedding to avoid conflict in the use of the sanctuary.

5. If the reception is to be held in the church, the room for this should be reserved.

6. Confer with the Minister of Music or choir director and the organist regarding both instrumental and vocal music to be used.

7. A kneeling bench, or pillow, should be provided in line with the dramatics of the ceremony. The usual questions, more or less common to every ceremony, will be asked of course. If you will read the ceremonies in use among the various faiths of Protestantism, also the Jewish and Catholic faiths, you will discover a striking similarity.

8. Books of etiquette, such as those prepared by *Vogue* or Amy Vanderbilt, offer expert guidance in marriage ceremony routine before, during and after the service itself, whether it takes place in a residence or a church. The Embassy Publishing Company, Inc., 33 West 42nd Street, New York, issues a Wedding Embassy Year Book offering expert guidance.

9. Customs, courtesies and traditions are all given ample consideration in books of etiquette. If a church wedding is contemplated, there are certain definite regulations to guide marriage preparations, the ceremony and the reception, and courtesies (to minister, organist and soloist).

II. The Rehearsal

To make sure that the joy and beauty of the occasion are preserved, at least one rehearsal should be planned when all parties concerned can be present. This will place everyone at ease when the time of the wedding arrives. If a rehearsal dinner is given it should be served after the rehearsal rather than before. Where the church employs a trained hostess she will take charge of all of these details, also at the wedding and the reception. This is her job. It's no job for a novice.

III. Decorations

Of course, the bride is primarily responsible for the decorations. She should manage this matter to include due attention to these items:

1. Installation and removal of decorations must not interfere with other uses of the church.
2. No decoration of any kind is to be placed on the Altar or the Communion Table, and no decorations should obscure the view of the Christian symbols.
3. No damage is in any way to be done to any portion of the church house.

IV. The Wedding

The wedding ceremony is fully covered in the wide range of choice offered in this Manual. The order of procedure will usually follow like this —

Preliminary Organ Music
Arrival of the Guests
Seating of the Groom's Parents and the
    Bride's Mother
Lighting of the Candles (see note below)
Musical Selections
The Wedding March, and Processional
    The Minister
    The Groom and Best Man
    The Bride's Party
The Wedding Ceremony
The Recessional

Votive lights are advised, in which event it will be unnecessary to arrange for the candle lighting. Where it is customary to have two lighted candles on the

Communion Table they should be lighted ahead of time for they are not a part of the ceremony.

In planning a church wedding the two diagrams, (1) The Procession and (2) The Recession, will be found serviceable. These two diagrams have been taken from *A Minister's Service Manual* by S. W. Hutton. They may be adjusted to suit desire and local personnel.

The following details should be talked over by the minister and the contracting parties ahead of time so that all movements and the dramatics, so full of meaning and yet simple, may be carried through with dignity and due solemnity.

At the appointed hour, while the ushers are walking down the aisle, the minister enters from a door just off the chancel and takes his position before the altar. In some churches the pulpit is in the center, and the service may be read from the pulpit or from the floor immediately in front of the pulpit. The bridegroom follows the minister and along with the best man will stand not far from the minister.

The bride and groom meet in front of the altar. The chosen ceremony will follow through according to guiding sentences from this point forward. (See next chapter for the ring in the wedding ceremony.)

Where a qualified hostess is available she will engineer the entire procedure including rehearsal, wedding and reception.

V. Photographs

It is a worthy custom to preserve a visible record of the marriage ceremony in the form of photographs. Some of these can be taken before the ceremony, or may be posed for after the marriage has been solemnized. There should be no delay in getting to the reception where guests are waiting. It is possible that a photo of the groom and the minister may be taken in the minister's study as the certificate is being signed. There is a possibility, where a photographer can be fully trusted, that a time exposure may be taken during the ceremony, but absolutely no flash bulbs are to be used during the ceremony. The photographer must keep out of sight.

VI. Fees

The fees should be agreed upon ahead of time as a rule. They should:

1. Include a different rate for communicants and those who are non-communicants.

2. Include these items as a matter of courtesy —
   The services of the minister
   The services of the church care-taker both for the wedding and the reception
   The use of the sanctuary or chapel
   The use of the room for the reception
   The musicians

VII. The Receiving Line at the Reception

Immediately inside the entrance of the room in which the reception is held the line may be formed as follows —

1. Mother of the Bride
2. Father of the Bride
3. Mother of the Groom
4. Father of the Groom
5. Bride and Groom (the Bride is to the right of the Groom)
6. Bridesmaids
7. Honor Attendant (Maid or Matron of Honor)

The Groomsman and the Ushers are not in the line.

Note: If a printed or mimeographed copy of Wedding Etiquette is desired it may be placed in the hands of all concerned.

CHAPTER 4

THE RING IN THE WEDDING CEREMONY

In the larger number of marriage services in this manual, the use of the ring is included. The ring is carried by the best man and is handed to the minister on request at the moment it is needed in the ceremony. The minister speaks a few words regarding the symbolism represented in the ring. He then hands it to the groom who places it on the third finger of the bride's left hand.

In marriages of today the bride will also give a ring to the groom. It will be brought to the ceremony by the maid of honor. On request of the minister she will hand it to him, who after a few sentences of appropriate comment will hand it to the bride who will place it on the ring finger of the groom as directed by the minister. (One or both of these rings are often heirlooms. The minister could very appropriately call attention to this fact.) Some couples prefer a ceremony without the use of a ring, or rings.

The customary formula is included in the ceremony, more particularly where a Prayer Book is used. However, it is possible for the minister as a rule to use his own initiative in making this part of the ceremony a beautifully expressed portion to enhance the meaning of the ring and the double ring ceremony.

(When the ring is handed to the minister he may say:)

"May this beautiful token and pledge symbolize the purity and endlessness of your love."

(Then the groom or bride will place the ring and repeat the following sentence after the minister:)

"This ring I give to you, in token and pledge, of our constant faith, and abiding love."

21

(The minister may then speak as follows:)

"Inasmuch as you have agreed together to enter the holy rite of wedlock, and have given and received a ring in token and in pledge of your love, I now declare you husband and wife in the name of Christ our Lord and Master."

(A prayer will close the ceremony.)

CHAPTER 5

MUSIC FOR CHURCH WEDDING CEREMONIES

It stands to reason that the music, both vocal and instrumental, for weddings solemnized in the church should be appropriate, not too sentimental but of the highest order. The following suggestions are offered for your consideration —

ORGAN MUSIC —

Bach, Johann Sebastian — "Prelude in G Major," and "Fugue from the Tocatta and Fugue in C"

Guilmant, Alexandre — "Nuptial March in E Major," and "Postlude Nuptiale"

"Wedding Music," Part I and Part II —
Published by General Service Music, Concordia Publishing House, St. Louis, Missouri

VOCAL MUSIC —

Bach, Johann Sebastian — "My Heart Ever Faithful" (from the Pentecost Cantata)

Bitgood, Roberta — "The Greatest of These Is Love" H. W. Grav Company, Inc., New York

Black, Jennie Prince — "The Pledge" G. Shirmer, Inc., New York

Blomfield, D. S. (words), Oscar Fox (music) — "O Perfect Love"

Charles, Ernest — "Love Is of God" G. Shirmer, Inc., New York

Diggle, Roland — "A Wedding Prayer" G. Shirmer, Inc., New York

Dunlap, Vern Glasgo — "Wedding Prayer" G. Shirmer, Inc., New York

Gounod, Charles Francois — "Entreat Me Not to Leave Thee"

Lesser, Rena Silverman — "God Bless This Day"

Lovelace, Austin — "We Lift Our Hearts to Thee," and "A Wedding Benediction"
G. Shirmer, Inc., New York

Malotte, Albert Hay — "The Lord's Prayer"
G. Shirmer, Inc., New York

HYMNS —

One or more stanzas of the following hymns are suitable for use as solos or choir numbers —

Baker-Palmer — "Jesus, Thou Joy of Loving Hearts" (Tune, Quebec)

Barnby — "O Perfect Love" (Tune by same name)

Barnby-Finlater — "O Happy Home, Where Thou Art Loved the Dearest" (Tune, Alverstroke)

Cruger-Winkworth — "Now Thank We All Our God" (Tune, *Nun Danket*)

Holmes, John Haynes — "O Father, Thou Who Givest All" (Tune, *O Jesu Christe, Wahres Licht*)

Knecht-Brooker — "Let the Whole Creation Cry" (Tune, Vienna)

Lloyd-Guiterman — "Bless the Four Corners of This House" (Tune, Abergele)

Chapter 6

A CONTINUING HOME MINISTRY

One of the most significant and fruitful fields of service for a minister is in the days, months and years following the marriage ceremony. When the ceremony has been concluded and the appropriate reception is over, the work of the minister has just begun. Even after he has extended his personal congratulations to the couple and the guests at the reception, he may quietly step aside and fill out an attractive wedding booklet which contains the marriage certificate. These booklets may be ordered from the publisher of your religious faith or from a local book store. It may be possible for the couple to choose the one they desire during the pre-marital period of counseling. These booklets range from a very simple type to the most elaborate. Guiding suggestions on this point should include simplicity and beauty.

The minister will make a brief record of the marriage for his own use, including by all means, if possible, the address and telephone number of the couple. He should promptly sign the license and return it to the office of the clerk who issued it so that the record of the marriage may be on file. There can be no reason for delay.

It is quite appropriate for the minister to suggest the observance of wedding anniversaries. The twenty-fifth and the fiftieth anniversaries may be enriched by repeating the original service with appropriate comments by the minister to make the occasion memorable and rich with wholesome sentiment. Repeating the original vows is heart-searching. For convenience, a list of anniversaries from one to sixty is provided (see page 31) to guide the minister in suggesting appropriate gifts which friends may bring to the occasion.

The minister can very acceptably send a card of greeting and remembrance to the couple on the first anniversary of their marriage. This first anniversary is very important in the lives of those who are married.

When a child is born, a card of blessing and greeting may be sent. Some ministers write a letter to the little one giving full instructions on how to bring up his parents, how to become a bonafide member of his household in growing teeth, learning to talk, to walk and to avoid getting his days and nights mixed. Sense and nonsense may be mingled in due proportions in such a letter. A service of blessing for parents and child may be planned for some Sunday morning as a part of the regular order of worship. (Your publisher will have these services which may be used and then given to the couple for their memory book.)

When the couple has moved into a home of their own or just finished paying for their own home, a very meaningful home dedication can be arranged. Here is a brief outline of such a service. The idea is becoming more and more popular. Such a service may be set up under the guidance of your Christian Education Committee. Provide for the whole family to participate, including grandparents and other relatives. They will never forget it. Such a dedication could be arranged at Christmas time or during National Family Week in May.

CHAPTER 7

A HOME DEDICATION SERVICE

INTRODUCTORY STATEMENT: (The Minister)

Jesus was born in Bethlehem of Judea. He shared three homes during the brief thirty-three years of his sojourn on earth. His childhood and youth were spent in the village of Nazareth. When he was rejected in Nazareth during the early days of his ministry, the family moved to Capernaum where he made headquarters during the larger part of his ministry. His third home was with his three close friends — Mary, Martha and Lazarus — at Bethany near Jerusalem. Today he seeks to share in your home and mine. Today we dedicate this home by turning first of all to the family Bible.

SCRIPTURE READING

Home Circles in Bible times
1. Ruth and Naomi — Ruth 1:1-18
2. Mary and Martha — Luke 10:38-42

HYMN:

(An appropriate hymn may be read or sung. The words may be printed in the dedication folder if one is used. A well-arranged order of procedure and worship should be provided. The following hymns are Numbers 599, 600, 601, 602 in *Christian Worship, a Hymnal* — Bethany Press, St. Louis, Missouri.)

"Bless the Four Corners of This House" — Guiterman-Lloyd

"O Father, Thou Who Givest All" — Holmes-Anonymous

Note: The above Home Dedication Service is an adaptation of a service beginning on page 55 of *Dedication Services* by S. W. Hutton, Baker Book House, Grand Rapids, Michigan, 1964.

A Home Dedication Service in completed form by S. W. Hutton, may be purchased for 50c through the Bethany Press, P.O. Box 179, St. Louis, Missouri 63166.

"O Happy Home, Where Thou Art Loved the Dearest" —
Findlater-Barnby

"Thou Gracious God Whose Mercy Lends"—Holmes-Joseph.

PRAYER: (By a Home-Maker of your choice)

Grant Thy special blessing on this home today, our Father, as we gather to dedicate this earthly dwelling of this family. May our thoughts be turned toward appreciation for the blessings that attend us along life's way, and may we all so live that we may be ready to meet our Maker in the heavenly home when we are called away from this habitation. We pray in the name of Christ who shared in home life among those He loved. Amen.

CEREMONY OF LIGHT AND FIRE

(While the mother in the household lights the candles, symbols of home cheer, someone says:)

There are many lights of home, but love that goes from heart to heart is the brightest of them all.

(After the candles have been lighted, someone continues:)

Love is an incense from an altar bright
Where candles shine with clear and mellow light;
It is a lamp that cheers us when we roam,
And a kindly spark that lights the fires of home.

(If there is a fireplace, let the husband light the fire, as the wife reads:)

"Kneel always when you light a fire
To God for his unfailing charity."

—John Oxenham

A TOUCH OF BEAUTY AND REMEMBRANCE

(Unveiling of pictures, paintings, tapestries or heirlooms with brief mention of each.)

DEDICATION RITUAL

Husband: We humbly dedicate this house with sincere appreciation of its builders, and with deep gratitude to God for our home.

Wife: We dedicate the doors of our home to hospitality and security.

Husband: We dedicate the windows that our home may be lighted and cheerful, and that we may look out on others with kindness and neighborliness.

Wife: We dedicate our furniture and all other home equipment with thoughts of consideration for all who have contributed to our comfort.

Husband: We dedicate our books in which our many friends, through the printed page, contribute much to our enlightment and enjoyment. Our magazines we also dedicate, for they help to keep us abreast of the times in which we live.

Wife: We dedicate our pictures and tapestries as symbols of beauty, friendship, hallowed memories and thoughtfulness.

Husband: We dedicate this home to love and wholesome companionship, to courage and patience, to courtesy and mutual helpfulness, to loyalty and human dignity.

Wife: We dedicate this home to work and leisure, to serious thinking, to gaiety and laughter, to music and restful relaxation.

Husband: We dedicate the lives within this home to the service of God and our fellowmen, a small unit of God's kingdom on earth, in which we are privileged to live. May we live worthily.

All: Together we share in this home dedication today in the spirit of love and goodwill.

PRAYER OF DEDICATION: (The Minister)

SOLO: "Bless This House" — Brahe

CLOSING PRAYER: (Everyone participating)
God be gracious to us and bless us
and make his face to shine upon us,

that thy way may be known upon earth,
    Thy saving power among all nations.
Let the people praise thee, O God;
    Let all the people praise thee.

— Psalm 67:1-3

MUSIC: (Both instrumental and vocal in good fellowship)

CHAPTER 8

A LIST OF MARRIAGE ANNIVERSARIES WITH APPROPRIATE GIFT SUGGESTIONS

This list of anniversaries with the customary gift suggestions will serve as a reference for the minister himself as he follows through in his ministry after he has married a couple. The minister may be asked for this information to meet a planned observance someone may have in mind.

First: paper
Second: cotton
Third: leather
Fourth: books
Fifth: wooden (clocks)
Sixth: iron
Seventh: copper, bronze or brass
Eighth: electrical appliances
Ninth: pottery
Tenth: tin, aluminum
Eleventh: steel
Twelfth: silk or linen
Thirteenth: lace
Fourteenth: ivory
Fifteenth: crystal
Twentieth: china
Twenty-fifth: silver
Thirtieth: pearl
Thirty-fifth: coral or jade
Fortieth: ruby
Forty-fifth: sapphire
Fiftieth: gold
Fifty-fifth: emerald
Sixtieth: diamond

The number of couples who have been married fifty years or more has increased quite noticeably in recent years. An annual party for couples who have been married fifty years or more is frequently given by some interested as daily paper or a church affiliated group. In these gat a prize is usually given to the couple married the longest. The minister would do well to help in the planning for these occasions and to participate in them.

National Family Week in May would be a very appropriate time to give emphasis to the years of marriage. It would be quite appropriate to set up a gathering known as *"The Festival of the Christian Home"* during the first week of May.

It may also be possible to fit this into this observance, The Dedication of a Home.

Chapter 9

MARRIAGE LAWS AS OF JANUARY 1, 1959

State or other jurisdiction	Age at which marriage can be contracted with parental consent		Age below which parental consent is required		Common-law marriage recognized	Physical examination and blood test for male and female		Waiting period	
	Male	Female	Male	Female		Time limit between examination and issuance of marriage license	Scope of medical examination	Before issuance of license	After issuance of license
Alabama	17	14	21	18	★	30 da.	(a)	......	......
Alaska	18(b)	16(b)	21	18	......	30 da.	(a)	3 da.	......
Arizona	18(c)	16(c)	21	18	......	30 da.	(a)	3 da.	......
Arkansas	18	16	21	18	......	30 da.	(a)	3 da.	......
California	18(b,d)	16(b,d)	21	18	★	30 da.	(a)	......	......
Colorado	16(b)	16(b)	21	18	......	30 da.	(a)	4 da.	......
Connecticut	16(b)	16(b)	21	21	......	40 da.	(a)	......	(e)
Delaware	18(c,d)	16(c)	21	18	★★	30 da.	(a)	3 da.	......
Florida	18(c,d)	16(c,d)	21	21	★★	30 da.	(a)	3 da.(h)	......
Georgia	(f)	14	17(g)	18(g)	★	30 da.	(a)	3 da.	......
Hawaii	18	16(b)	20	18	......	30 da.	(a)	......	......
Idaho	15	15(b)	18	18	★★	30 da.	(a)	......	......
Illinois	18(c)	16	21	18	......	15 da.	(a)	3 da.	......
Indiana	18(c)	16(c)	21	18	......	30 da.	(a)	3 da.	......
Iowa	16	14	21	18	★★	20 da.	(a,i)	3 da.	......
Kansas	16	14	21	21	★★	30 da.	(a)	3 da.	......
Kentucky	16	16(b)	21	21	......	15 da.	(a)	3 da.	72 hrs.
Louisiana	16(b)	16(b)	21	18	......	10 da.	(a)	......	......
Maine	16(b)	16(b)	21	18	......	30 da.	(a)	5 da.	......
Maryland	18(c)	16(c)	21	18	......	30 da.	(a)	48 hrs.	......
Massachusetts	18(b)	16(b)	21	18	......	30 da.	(a)	5 da.	......
Michigan	(f)	16(c)	18	18	......	30 da.	(a)	3 da.	......
Minnesota	18(b)	16(b)	21	18	......	30 da.	(a)	5 da.	......
Mississippi	17(b)	15(b)	21	21	★	30 da.	(a)	3 da.	......
Missouri	15(b)	15(b)	21	18	......	15 da.	(a)	3 da.	......
Montana	18	16	21	21	......	20 da.	(a)	......	......
Nebraska	18	16	21	21	......	30 da.	(a)	......	......
Nevada	18	16	21	18	......	......	......	......	......

State	Age with consent	Without consent	Without consent	Blood test	Diseases	Exam valid	Waiting period
New Hampshire	(j)	20	18		(a)	30 da.	5 da.
New Jersey	16(b)	21	18		(a)	30 da.	72 hrs.
New Mexico	18(c)	21	18		(a)	30 da.	
New York	16	21	18		(a)	30 da.	24 hrs.(k)
North Carolina	16(c)	18	18		(l)	30 da.	(m)
North Dakota	18	21	18		(n)	30 da.	
Ohio	18	21	21	★★	(a)	30 da.	5 da.
Oklahoma	15(c)	18	18		(a)	30 da.(o)	
Oregon	18	21	15		(p)	30 da.	3 da.
Pennsylvania	16(b)	21	18		(a)	30 da.	3 da.
Rhode Island	18(b)	21	21	★★★★	(q)	40 da.	(r)
South Carolina	14	18	18				24 hrs.
South Dakota	15	18	18	★	(a)	20 da.	3 da.(s)
Tennessee	16(b)	21	18		(a)	30 da.	
Texas	14	21	18		(a)	15 da.	
Utah	16(d)	21	18		(a)	30 da.	5 da.
Vermont	16(b)	21	18		(a)	30 da.	
Virginia	18(c,d)	21	21		(a)	30 da.	
Washington	(t)	21	18		(a)	30 da.	
West Virginia	16(d)	21	21		(a)	30 da.	3 da.
Wisconsin	15	18	18		(a)	15 da.	3 da.
Wyoming	16	21	21		(a)	30 da.	5 da.
District of Columbia	18	21	18	★			3 da.

*Prepared by the Women's Bureau, United States Department of Labor.

(a) Venereal diseases.
(b) In special circumstances statute establishes procedure whereby younger parties may obtain license.
(c) Statute establishes procedure whereby younger parties may obtain license in case of pregnancy or birth of a child.
(d) Parental consent is not required if minors were previously married.
(e) Residents, 24 hours; non-residents, 96 hours.
(f) No provision in law for parental consent for males.
(g) If parties are under 21, notice must be posted unless parent of female consents in person.
(h) Unless parties are 21 years or more, or female is pregnant.
(i) Feeblemindedness.
(j) Below age of consent parties need parental consent and permission of judge.
(k) Marriage may not be solemnized within 3 days from date on which specimen for serological test was taken.
(l) Epilepsy, idiocy, imbecility, mental defectiveness, unsound mindedness, tuberculosis and venereal diseases.
(m) 48 hours if both are non-residents.
(n) Feeblemindedness, imbecility, insanity, chronic alcoholism and venereal diseases.
(o) Time limit between date of examination and expiration of marriage license.
(p) Venereal diseases, epilepsy, feeblemindedness, mental illness, drug addiction and chronic alcoholism.
(q) Tuberculosis and venereal diseases.
(r) If female is non-resident, must complete and sign license 5 days prior to marriage.
(s) Does not apply when parties are over 21 years of age.
(t) No minimum age set.

From Book of the States 1961-62; with permission of the Council of State Governments.

CHAPTER 10

GROUNDS FOR DIVORCE

(From Table IX, "The Law of Marriage and Divorce," by Kuchler — Oceana Publications, Inc., 80 Fourth Avenue, New York 3, New York

ADULTERY: Everywhere

ATTEMPT ON LIFE OF OTHER SPOUSE: Ill., Ia., Ky., La., Mont., Pa., Tenn.

ATTEMPT TO PROSITUTE WIFE: Puerto Rico

CRUELTY (EXTREME): In all states except Ala., Alas., Hawaii, Md., N.C., N.Y., Va., D.C., Puerto Rico

CONVICTION FOR FELONY: Ala., Alas., Ariz., Ark., Cal., Conn., Del., Ga., Hawaii, Ida., Ill., Ind., Ia., Kan., Ky. La., Md., Mass., Mich., Minn., Miss., Mont., Nebr., Nev., N.D., N.H., N.M., Ohio, Okla., Ore., Pa., R.I., S.D., Tenn., Tex., Utah, Vt., Va., Wash., W. Va., Wis., Wyo., D.C., Puerto Rico, Virgin Islands

DEFAMATION OF OTHER SPOUSE: La., Mont.

DESERTION: In all states except N.C. and N.Y., also Puerto Rico

DISAPPEARANCE: Conn., N.H., Vt., N.Y.

DIVORCE OUT OF STATE BY OTHER PARTY: Fla., Mich., Ohio

FORCE OR DURESS: Ga., Ky., Pa., Wash.

FRAUD: Conn., Ga., Kan., Ohio, Okla., Pa., Wash.

HABITUAL DRUNKENNESS: Ala., Alas., Ariz., Ark., Cal., Colo., Conn., Del., Fla., Ga. Hawaii, Ida., Ill., Ind., Ia., Kan., Ky., La., Mass., Mich., Minn., Miss., Mo., Mont., Nebr., Nev., N.D., N.H., Ohio, Okla., Ore., R.I., S.C.,

S.D., Tenn., Utah, Wash., W. Va., Wis., Wyo., Puerto Rico, Virgin Islands

HABITUAL USE OF DRUGS: Ala., Colo., Fla., Hawaii, Me., Miss., R.I., W. Va., Puerto Rico

IDIOCY OR INSANITY: Ala., Alas., Ark., Cal., Colo., Del., Hawaii, Ida., Ind., Kan., Ky., Md., Minn., Miss., Mont., Nebr., Nev., N.C., N.D., N.M., Okla., Ore., S.D., Tex., Utah, Vt., Wash., Wyo., Puerto Rico, Virgin Islands

IMPOTENCE: Ala., Alas., Ariz., Ark., Colo., Fla., Ga., Ill., Ind., Kan., Ky., Mass., Me., Md., Mo., Nebr., Nev., N.C., N.H., N.M., Ohio, Pa., R.I., Tenn., Utah, V., Wash., Wis., Wyo., Puerto Rico

INCEST: Fla., Ga., Miss., Pa., R.I.

INCOMPATIBILITY: Alas., N.M., Okla., Virgin Islands

INDIGNITIES: Ariz., Ark., Hawaii, Ky., Mo., Mont., Ore., Pa., Wash., Wyo.

JOINING SECT BELIEVING COHABITATION UNLAWFUL: Ky., N.H.

LIVING APART: Ala., Ariz., Ida., Ky., La., Md., Minn., Nev., N.C., R.I., Tex., Utah, Vt., Wash., Wis., Wyo., D.C., Puerto Rico

MALFORMATION PREVENTING SEXUAL INTERCOURSE: Ky.

MENTAL INCAPACITY: Ga., Miss.

NON-SUPPORT BY HUSBAND: Alas., Ariz., Colo., Del., Hawaii, Ida., Ind., Mass., Me., Mont., Nebr., Nev., N.D., N.H., N.M., Ohio, Okla., R.I., S.D., Tenn., Utah, Vt., Wash., Wis., Wyo.

PRIOR MARRIAGE: Ark., Colo., Del., Fla., Ill., Kan., Miss., Mo., Ohio, Okla., Pa., R.I., Tenn.

REFUSAL BY WIFE TO MOVE TO NEW RESIDENCE: Tenn.

REFUSAL TO COHABIT: N.H.

UNCHASTITY (WIFE'S): Ky., Va.

UNDER AGE OF CONSENT: R.I.

UNNATURAL BEHAVIOR: Ala., N.C., Tenn.

VAGRANCY: Mo., Wyo.

VENEREAL DISEASE: Ill., Hawaii, Ky.

VIOLENT TEMPER: Ala., Alas., Ariz., Fla., Ky., La., Mich., Mont., Nebr., Tenn., Tex., Wis.

WIFE PREGNANT AT MARRIAGE: Ala., Ariz., Ga., Kan., Ky., Miss., Mo., N.C., N.M., Okla., Tenn., Va., Wyo.

WILFUL NEGLECT: Alas., Cal., Conn., Ida., Kan., Ky., Mass., Me., Mich., Mont., Nebr., Nev., N.D., Ohio, Okla., R.I., S.D., Tenn., Utah, Vt., Wash., Wis., Wyo.

Note: Credit is hereby given to Dr. Kuchler, author, and the Oceana Publications, Inc., Dobbs Ferry, New York, 10522 for permission to use the above "Grounds for Divorce" arranged by subjects. This same company has also issued a book bearing the title *The Law of Engagement and Marriage*. Separation and Divorce will be treated in a separate book.

CHAPTER 11

A SCRIPTURAL MARRIAGE CEREMONY

(Some ministers from non-liturgical faiths may desire a brief Scriptural ceremony. Here is one which will serve as a foundation on which the minister may build an enriched, heart-searching ceremony using his own initiative. At times the couple to be married may request a Scriptural service.)

DEARLY BELOVED, we are assembled here in the presence of God and this company of loved ones and friends, to join this man and this woman in the bonds of holy matrimony. The Scriptures challenge us with the sacredness of the Marriage relation and set forth the love of Christ for his Church as an example of deepest devotion. The Master himself shared the joys of the Marriage Feast in Galilee. In the first Corinthian letter, the great Apostle very beautifully guides us in the underlying meaning of love —

"Love is patient and kind;
Love is not jealous or boastful;
Love is not arrogant or rude;
Love does not insist on its own way;
It does not rejoice at wrong, but rejoices in the right.
Love bears all things, believes all things, hopes all
    things, endures all things.
Love never ends."

— I Corinthians 13:4-8a

A union setting forth such an ideal is not to be entered into hastily or without due consideration, but reverently, discretely, advisedly and in the fear of our Heavenly Father. If either of you or anyone in this assembly knows any just cause why this marriage should not be performed, let him speak now, or hereafter hold his peace.

(Then shall the minister say to the groom:)

Do you, _____, take this woman to be your lawful wedded wife, to love and respect her, honor and cherish her, in health and in sickness, in prosperity and in adversity; and leaving all others to keep yourself only unto her, so long as you both shall live?

(The groom replies:)

I do.

(Then shall the minister say to the bride:)

Do you, _____, in like manner solemnly agree to receive this man as your lawful wedded husband, to love and respect him, and to live with him in all faith and tenderness, in health and in sickness, in prosperity and in adversity, and leaving all others to keep yourself unto him, so long as you both shall live?

(The bride replies:)

I do.

Have you a ring?

(The groom shall hand the ring to the minister, who may comment as he holds the ring:)

May this beautiful token and pledge symbolize the purity and never-ending love you have for your chosen companion in life.

(Then the minister will hand the ring to the groom, who will place it on the third finger of the bride and repeat after the minister these words:)

This ring I give to you / in token and pledge / of our constant faith, / and abiding love.

(In the event the bride also has a ring for the groom, the same routine may be followed.)

(Then the minister shall say:)

Inasmuch as you have agreed to enter the marriage relationship, and have given and received a ring(s) in token of your faith, I now, by the authority committed unto me as a minister of the gospel, declare that _____ and _____ are husband and wife according to the ordinance of God and the law of the State.

(Then the minister shall offer a prayer:)

Heavenly Father, we have heard from these two people the impressive acceptance of the solemn and significant vows of marriage. Do Thou grant unto them grace and courage, love and loyalty, constancy and faith to maintain these vows to the end of the way.

May this new home radiate the sunshine of Thy love, and may everyone who comes in contact with this home be enriched and ennobled. Through Christ who shares in this sacred institution we pray. Amen.

———

Note: This Scriptural marriage ceremony is patterned after a similar ceremony by the Reverend Neil Crawford in the *Cokesbury Marriage Manual*, page 59-62.

CHAPTER 12

A BRIEF MARRIAGE CEREMONY

(The minister says to the guests:)

When Jesus was called to the marriage at Cana of Galilee, he gladly joined the happy company and there began his ministry and acts of power. Since that day the entrance of the Christ into homes which bid him welcome has been the occasion of rich blessing, of spiritual strength and the increase of joy. Desiring his companionship at the outset of their wedded life, this man and this woman have called us to be witnesses before our Lord of the pledges they are about to make to each other, and to set them forth in their new estate by our prayers and Christian greetings.

(To the parties the minister says:)

This rite of marriage in which you now come to be united is the first and oldest rite of mankind. Marriage is our foretaste of Paradise, given in the wisdom of God to soothe the troubles and increase the joys of our earthly life. This it will do for you, if you purpose in your hearts to beautify and sweeten it by your tender devotions, your mindfulness in little things, your patience and sacrifice of self to each other. Coming in full love to the threshold of a new life together, I commend to you these spiritual ministries as the way to lasting happiness.

(To the man the minister shall say:)

Will you, _____, take this woman to be your wedded wife, promising to keep, cherish, and defend her and to be her faithful and true husband so long as you both shall live?

(The groom replies:)

I will.

(To the woman the minister shall say:)

Will you, _____, take this man to be your wedded husband, promising to adhere unalterably to him in all life's changes, and to be his loving and true wife till death divide you?

(The bride replies:)

I will.

(The ring for the bride is secured by the minister:)

In the providence of God, and for the fullest happiness of the home, there are ways in which the husband is the head of the wife. He imparts unto her his name, and receives her into his care and protection — in token of which he gives her this ring in pledge.

Thus are you to compass about her life with strength and protecting love.

Thus are you to wear this ring as the enclosing bond of reverence and dearest faith — both fulfilling the perfect circle of duty that makes you one.

(The ring is given to the groom, who places it on the bride's finger, and repeats after the minister:)

I, _____, take thee, _____, to be my wedded wife, to have and to hold from this day forward, for better, for worse, for richer, for poorer, in sickness and in health, to love and to cherish until death us do part.

(The ring for the groom is secured by the minister:)

Because the man becomes to the woman her companion in all of life's experience, and is henceforth distinguished by his devotion to her, he wears this ring as the mark of his faithfulness.

(The ring is given to the woman, who places it on the man's finger, and repeats after the minister:)

I, _____, take thee, _____, to be my wedded husband, to have and to hold from this day forward, for better, for worse, for richer, for poorer, in sickness and in health, to love and to cherish until death us do part.

(The pronouncement)

Forasmuch as this man and this woman have promised to be faithful and true to each other, and have witnessed the same before God and this company by spoken vows and by giving and receiving rings in pledge, they enter now into a new estate. As a minister of Jesus Christ, I pronounce them husband and wife. What God has joined together, let no man put asunder.

(The prayer)

Our Father in heaven, we pray that the coming of this couple unto one who represents for them the ministry of the Lord Jesus Christ may be but a sign and a promise of their coming unto thee in all of the high experiences of life. May thy blessing rest upon the union which is formed here this hour, we pray in the name of Jesus Christ. Amen.

Note: Ministers of the Christian Church (Disciples) are at liberty to use any wording of their choice in the solemnization of marriage. This ceremony was composed and used by Dr. A. T. DeGroot, Distinguished Professor of Church History, Brite Divinity School, Texas Christian University, for the marriage of two students.

CERTIFICATE

This is to certify that the foregoing ceremony of marriage was read by me for the parties indicated ....

....

at .... (City and State)

on .... (Date)

Signed ....

Minister of the Christian Church

Note: The actual copy of the ceremony, including the certificate, will be handed to the couple after the ceremony.

Chapter 13

A MARRIAGE CEREMONY INCLUDED WITHIN A COMPLETE ORDER OF WORSHIP

(Arranged for a Church Wedding)

PRELUDE

CALL TO WORSHIP: (The Minister)

The Call to Worship is a call to decide whom we will worship.

PRAYER: (The Minister)

Almighty God, unto whom all hearts are open, all desires known, and from whom no secrets are hid; cleanse the thoughts of our hearts by the inspiration of the Holy Spirit, that we may perfectly love thee, and worthily magnify thy holy name, through Christ our Lord. Amen.

HYMN: "Praise to the Lord"

THE SERVICE OF CONFESSION: (The Minister)

Confession is the act whereby we acknowledge our sinful past and receive God's judgment and forgiveness.

SCRIPTURE SENTENCES: (All standing)

THE CALL TO CONFESSION: (The Minister)

Let us humbly confess our sins unto almighty God.

PRAYER OF GENERAL CONFESSION: (The congregation, seated.)

Almighty and most merciful Father, we have erred and strayed from thy ways like lost sheep. We have followed too much the devices and desires of our own hearts. We have offended against thy holy laws. We have left undone those things which we ought to have done; and we have done those things which we ought not to have done; and there is no health in us. But thou, O Lord, have mercy upon us, miserable offenders. Spare thou those, O God, who confess their faults. Restore thou those who are penitent; according to thy promises declared unto mankind in Christ Jesus our Lord. And grant, O merciful Father, for his sake, That we may hereafter live a godly, righteous, and sober life, to the glory of thy holy Name. Amen.

The Assurance of Pardon: (The Minister)

Our Father has had mercy upon us as our fathers in the faith and the Holy Scriptures bear witness to us. Hear these words: in all these things we are more than conquerers through him who loved us. For I am sure that neither death, nor life, nor angels, nor principalities, nor things present, nor things to come, nor height, nor depth, nor anything else in all creation will be able to separate us from the love of God in Christ Jesus our Lord.

The Service of the Word

MINISTER: Having received God's judgment and forgiveness, we are able again to hear his living word in the present.

The congregation will stand.

MINISTER: O Lord, open thou our lips.

CONGREGATION: And our mouth shall show forth thy praise.

MINISTER: Glory be to the Father, and to the Son, and to the Holy Ghost;

CONGREGATION: As it was in the beginning, is now, and ever shall be, world without end. Amen.

MINISTER: Praise ye the Lord.

CONGREGATION: The Lord's name be praised.

OLD TESTAMENT LESSON: Song of Solomon 2:8-17 (The Minister; The congregation will be seated.)

RESPONSE: (The congregation will stand)

MINISTER: O come, let us sing to the Lord,

CONGREGATION: Let us make a joyful noise to the rock of our salvation.

MINISTER: Let us come into his presence with thanksgiving; let us make a joyful noise to him with songs of praise.

CONGREGATION: For the Lord is a great God, and a great King above all gods.

MINISTER: In his hand are the depths of the earth; the heights of the mountains are his also.

CONGREGATION: The sea is his, for he made it; and his hands formed the dry land.

MINISTER: O come, let us worship and bow down, let us kneel before the Lord, our Maker.

CONGREGATION: For he is our God, and we are the people of his pasture, and the sheep of his hand.

MINISTER: Worship the Lord in holy array; tremble before him all the earth.

CONGREGATION: For he comes, for he comes to judge the earth. He will judge the world with righteousness, and the peoples with his truth.

(From Psalms 95 and 96)

MINISTER: Glory be to the Father, and to the Son, and to the Holy Ghost; as it was in the beginning, is now, and ever shall be, world without end. Amen.

THE NEW TESTAMENT LESSON: I Corinthians 13:1-13 (The Minister; The congregation will be seated.)

RESPONSE: (The congregation will stand)

MINISTER: Lord, now lettest thou thy servant depart in peace, according to thy word.

CONGREGATION: For mine eyes have seen thy salvation.

MINISTER: Which thou hast prepared before the face of all people;

CONGREGATION: A light for revelation to the Gentiles, and for the glory to thy people Israel.

MINISTER: Glory be to the Father, and to the Son, and to the Holy Ghost; as it was in the beginning, is now, and ever shall be, world without end. Amen.

THE SERVICE OF DEDICATION: (The Minister; The congregation will be seated.)

Having confessed our sin and heard God's gracious word, we commit our lives to the future, confident of his care.

PROCESSIONAL: "Now Thank We All Our God" — Karg-Eilert

THE VOWS OF MARRIAGE:

(The marriage vows may be chosen from one of the ceremonies offered in this marriage manual. In any event these should be cleared with the bride and groom ahead of the ceremony that the entire service may flow forward smoothly.)

(At the conclusion of the vows the minister says:)

These vows, like all covenants, are an irrevocable commitment under God's judgment and love to a new order of life.

RECESSIONAL: "The Wedding March" — Mendelssohn

Note: Prepared by Faith and Life Community, Austin, Texas.

Chapter 14

A COMMUNION SERVICE TO BE INCLUDED WITHIN THE MARRIAGE CEREMONY

(To be used after the minister has pronounced the couple husband and wife.)

The gift of love is one of God's greatest gifts to man. Realizing its value, _____ and _____ have expressed their desire to always share their love in light of, and in obedience to, God's love for them.

As Christ said, "Do this in remembrance of me," it is altogether fitting that the first act of this couple as husband and wife should be their sharing in the Lord's Supper.

"The Lord on the night that he was betrayed took bread, and when he had given thanks, he broke it and said 'This is my body which is for you. Do this in remembrance of me.'

"In the same way also the cup, saying, 'This cup is the New Testament in my blood. Do this, as often as you drink it, in remembrance of me.' For as often as you eat this bread and drink the cup, you proclaim the Lord's death until he comes."

—I Corinthians 11:23-26

(The minister serves the bread and wine to the new husband and wife, then follows with the prayer and benediction.)

PRAYER:

Good Father of all mankind, the world and all that is therein, we are grateful for the lives of these two people and for the new home they are establishing today. The stars of love shine in their eyes; the depths of love are hidden in their hearts. May this union be blessed with continuing love and understanding through the years ahead, and may all of us here present today remember this lovely occasion and its deepest meanings. In the name and for the sake of Jesus who is called the Christ. Amen.

BENEDICTION:

> "The grace of the Lord Jesus Christ,
> and the love of God,
> and the fellowship of the Holy Spirit
> be with you all."
>
> —II Corinthians 13:14

PART II

SOURCE MATERIALS FOR MARRIAGE

(Various Marriage Ceremonies)

A Baptist Marriage Service

A Christian Church Marriage Ceremony

An Episcopal Marriage Service

A Lutheran Order for Marriage

The Marriage Service of the Methodist Church

The Presbyterian Marriage Ceremony

The Catholic Marriage Ceremony

A Jewish Marriage Service

CHAPTER 15

A BAPTIST MARRIAGE SERVICE

We are together in this holy and sacred hour to witness the uniting of these two devoted hearts in the enduring bonds of Christian marriage. This most blessed and lasting of human relationships was first celebrated in the quiet bowers of Eden, in the time of man's innocency. "God saw that it was not good for man to live alone." And so He created woman and gave her to him to be his companion, his wife. "And for this cause shall a man leave father and mother and shall cleave unto his wife. And they two shall be one flesh."

Who then, in the name of our Heavenly Father, doth give this woman to wed?

And now, (groom's full name) and (bride's full name), (groom's first name) and (bride's first name), having freely and deliberately and prayerfully chosen each other as partners for life, will you please unite your right hands.

(First name of groom), you are now entering a relationship with many privileges, but also many obligations. The woman you love is about to become your wife. In no way could she so tell of her love for you as by her willingness to turn from home and loved ones and friends, true and tried, to make her home with you. Your joys will be her joys and your sorrows her sorrows. Your people will be her people and your God her God.

(First name of bride), you, too, are entering into a relationship with many privileges and obligations. The man

55

you love is about to become your husband. He tells the world not only of his willingness but of his express desire to turn from all others and to you for all of life ahead. Your love will be his inspiration and your prayers his tower of strength.

And now, here in the presence of God and these witnesses, do you take each other as husband and wife, agreeing to love each other devotedly and to promote each other's happiness until this union into which you are entering is dissolved by death? Do you promise?

(Minister holds bride's ring) The ring has long been the symbol for the sealing of important contracts. In the earlier history of man, the king wore a ring upon which was pressed the seal of the kingdom. With this ring he stamped the treaties of his land. But in more recent generations, the ring has been used to seal the marriage contract.

The ring teaches us many lessons. The purity of its metal reminds us of the purity of your love for each other, and the circle reminds us of the eternity of your love, the circle having neither beginning nor end.

Will you take the ring, (first name of groom), and place it upon (first name of the bride)'s finger, and, as you do, repeat to her after me these words:

"With this ring I thee wed, and all my worldly goods I thee endow. In sickness and in health, in poverty or in wealth, till death do us part."

(First name of groom), it is (first name of bride)'s desire that you, too, shall wear a ring, a ring to remind you of the purity and the eternity of her love for you. As she places it upon your finger and as you wear it proudly before men, it will proclaim to all the world that you belong to God.

Will you, (first name of bride), place it upon (first (name of groom)'s finger, and, as you do, repeat to him after me these words:

56

"With this ring I thee wed and all my worldly goods I thee endow. In sickness and in health, in poverty or in wealth, till death do us part."

And now, having pledged your love for and loyalty to each other, and having sealed the pledge with the marriage rings, I do, by the authority vested in me as a minister in the church of the living God, and in conformity with the laws of this state, pronounce you husband and wife. "And what God hath joined together, let not man put asunder."

Let us pray:

Add thy blessings, our loving Heavenly Father, to this quiet service here in thy church where these two winsome young people, in whose hearts thou hast inspired a lasting love, have said the words that have made them one in the eyes of society. Bless them as they turn now to walk the path of life together. Give them thy guidance in every tender and intimate adjustment to living together.

Bestow upon them, we pray, the fulfillment of the dreams and prayers they have cherished through their days for their love and for their home. In the course of the years to come, if it is thy will, grant them the laughter of little children, the peace which passeth understanding at their fireside, and all of the things that make a house into a home.

Remind them, our Father, that loving thee does not take away from our love for each other. We know that loving thee but increases our capacity to love those who are dearest to us, for God is love.

Bless the homes from whence they have come, but especially bless the home that they establish, and may it fulfill thy purpose and thy will. In Jesus' name we pray. Amen.

Note: Prepared by Dr James G. Harris, Pastor, University Baptist Church, Fort Worth, Texas, and used with his permission.

CHAPTER 16

A CHRISTIAN CHURCH MARRIAGE CEREMONY*

(This ceremony has been developed across the years and is still being changed on occasions. It combines features borrowed from the Episcopal Ceremony and from other sources, together with original materials by Dr. Davis. With couples the minister knows well, brief remarks of a personal nature are included.)

AFTER THE BRIDE COMES TO THE ALTAR: (The minister speaks)

"The Lord is in His holy temple. Let all the earth keep silence before him."

My dear friends, in the presence of God and before these witnesses, we have come together to unite in marriage _____ and _____.

Marriage is a divine institution, and we are taught in the Scriptures that it is to be honored among all men. Jesus himself honored marriage by performing his first miracle at the wedding in Cana of Galilee, and God has always honored marriage.

(Then the minister, speaking to the bride and groom, will say):

I require and charge you both that the vows you take this day are sacred above words, and that your lives hereafter shall be bound together unbreakably. But the security of your marriage will not rest in the rite or ritual of any church, nor in the word of any priest or minister. The security of your marriage will rest in the true purposes of your hearts, in your character, in the steadfastness of your devotion and in the love of God.

---

*by Dr. George R. Davis, Minister, National City Christian Church, Washington, D.C.

(Then in turn the minister will address the groom and the bride, and each in turn will answer:)

Will you, _____, have _____, to be your wife, will you love her, honor her, comfort and keep her, and forsaking all others remain true to her as long as you both live? If so you may answer, "I will."

(Each in turn then answers, "I will.")

(After exchange of vows the minister will pray, including personal elements, but always these words:)

God our Father, upon these thy two children, _____ and _____, we pray thy blessing. Grant these moments to be so filled with divine and sacred meaning, that they may be able to look back on them through all the years to come, and know this was a good hour, through Jesus Christ our Lord. Amen.

(The minister then addresses the father of the bride, or that person who is to give the bride away:)

Who gives (the name is used here) to be married to (the name of the groom used here)?

(The answer is given, "I do," or "her mother and I," or whatever form has been agreed upon. In case the bride is not given away, the ceremony continues following the prayer, as follows:)

IF A DIVIDED CEREMONY IS BEING USED:

(The minister, the couple, the maid of honor and best man, move from the sanctuary level, into the chancel; the minister behind the kneeling bench, and the wedding party standing in front of it. In a small chapel wedding, or in a home, they remain in the same position, from the beginning. In some cases (where requested, even in small weddings) a kneeling bench is used, and the couple stand before it from the very beginning of the ceremony. In a church wedding where additional attendants are used, all but the four persons move into the chancel during the processional and remain there until the recessional. Only the bride and groom, maid of honor and best man, stand below the chancel for the opening part of the ceremony as suggested above.)

(When all have arrived before the kneeling bench, the minister says:)

Having chosen to declare your vows in this sacred place, may I remind you that the home existed before the church, and that the first churches met in homes. Here this day you establish a home. And though you are taught in our religion that, "a man shall forsake his father and mother and cleave to his wife," yet nevertheless, each of you brings to your marriage, background and memory, and keen appreciation for those you love, and by whose loyalty and concern you were made ready for life and life's blessings. If that has been sound and wholesome, you enter into this experience twice blessed. If you would consumate the purposes of your hearts as you stand before this alter, you will say after me,

> "I (here the name of the groom is used) take thee (and here the name of the bride is used) to be my wife, and before God and these witnesses I promise to be a faithful and true husband."

(The bride then repeats a like vow.)

(Then the minister addressing the groom says:)

Do you have a ring as a symbol of this marriage?

(The groom secures the ring from the best man and in turn presents it to the minister. The minister in turn says:)

Bless, O Lord, this ring that he who gives it and she who wears it may dwell in thy peace.

(On some occasions the minister may give a more elaborate statement concerning the symbolism of the ring, as a circle, representing dependable and faithful love.)

(The minister then returns the ring to the groom, and the groom in turn places it on the bride's finger saying:)

> With this ring, before God, I thee wed. I will love thee, I will cherish thee, I will not forsake thee, in the name of the Father, and of the Son, and of the Holy Spirit. Amen.

(The same ring ceremony is used with the bride, and her answers are the same.)

(The minister then asks the bride and groom to join right hands, and he says:)

Upon the taking of your vows and the giving and receiving of the rings, by God's authority, I declare you to be husband and wife. What God has joined together, man cannot cut assunder.

(On some occasions the Lord's Prayer is included here.)

(Then the minister asks the bride and groom to kneel for prayer. When they kneel the minister often says:)

Love each other dearly, for there is scarcely anything else in all the world than this.

(Then parts of I Corinthians are quoted. On some occasions the couple requests Communion, and they are served at this time while they are kneeling. Here the minister dwells on the centrality of Christ in the home and in all true love. The usual Scriptural verses are quoted then in reference to the Communion, and the minister serves the Communion and usually partakes with them.)

The Prayer Follows:

(The prayer always contains personal elements, is devotional and always includes the following) —

Grant thy blessing, O Father, upon these thy two children. Teach them so to live in this world according to all thy high laws that they may find happiness and usefulness together. Teach them to live in kindness, in patience, in love, always in the willingness to forgive, that they may find true happiness. Teach them so to live together that when they are together their love may be to them an inspiration, and when they are apart their love may be to them as a light in the darkness.

Teach them so to live together that they may have the blessing of life eternal, through Jesus Christ our Lord. Amen.

A Traditional Benediction:

May the Lord bless thee and keep thee,
may he cause his face to shine upon thee
and be gracious unto thee,

may he lift up the light of his countenance upon thee and grant thee peace. Amen.

SOLO: "The Lord's Prayer," by Brahe
(Use of this solo here is optional.)

RECESSIONAL:

Note: Much freedom is allowed in the ceremony here presented, and the minister always prepared some original brief sections for each ceremony but within the context of the general outline here given. Included in this Marriage Manual by permission of Dr. Davis, at this time Pastor of the President of the United States.

CHAPTER 17

AN EPISCOPAL MARRIAGE SERVICE

(At the day and time appointed for Solemnization of Matrimony, the persons to be married shall come in to the body of the church, or shall be ready in some proper house, with their friends and neighbors; and there standing together, the man on the right hand, and the woman on the left, the minister shall say:)

Dearly beloved, we are gathered together here in the sight of God, and in the face of this company, to join together this Man and this Woman in holy Matrimony: which is an honorable estate, instituted of God, signifying unto us the mystical union that is betwixt Christ and his Church; which holy estate Christ adorned and beautified with his presence and first miracle that he wrought in Cana of Galilee, and is commended of Saint Paul to be honourable among all men: and therefore is not by any to be entered into unadvisedly or lightly; but reverently, discreetly, advisedly, soberly, and in the fear of God. Into this holy estate these two persons present come now to be joined. If any man can show just cause, why they may not lawfully be joined together, let him now speak, or else hereafter forever hold his peace.

And, also, speaking unto the persons who are to be married, he shall say:

I require and charge you both, as ye will answer at the dreadful day of judgment, when the secrets of all hearts shall be disclosed, that if either of you know any impediment why ye may not be lawfully joined together in matrimony, ye do now confess it. For be ye well assured, that if any persons are joined together otherwise than as God's Word doth allow, their marriage is not lawful.

The minister, if he shall have reason to doubt of the lawfulness of the proposed marriage, may demand sufficient surety for his indemnification; but if no impediment shall be alleged, or suspected, the minister shall say to the man:

—————————, wilt thou have this woman to thy wedded wife, to live together after God's ordinance, in the holy estate of matrimony? Wilt thou love her, comfort her, honour, and keep her, in sickness and in health; and, forsaking all others, keep thee only unto her, so long as ye both shall live?

The man shall answer,
I will.

Then shall the minister say unto the woman:

—————————, wilt thou have this man to thy wedded husband, to live together after God's ordinance, in the holy estate of matrimony? Wilt thou love him, comfort him, honour, and keep him, in sickness and in health; and, forsaking all others, keep thee only unto him, so long as ye both shall live?

The woman shall answer,
I will.

Then shall the minister say,
Who giveth this woman to be married to this man?

Then shall they give their Troth to each other in this manner. The minister, receiving the woman at her father's or friend's hands, shall cause the man with his right hand to take the woman by his right hand, and to say after him as followeth,

I —————————, take thee —————————, to my wedded wife, to have and to hold from this day forward, for better for worse, for richer for poorer, in sickness and in health, to love and to cherish, till death us do part, according to God's holy ordinance; and there to I plight thee my troth.

Then shall they loose their hands; and the woman, with her right hand take the man by his right hand, shall likewise say after the minister:

I—————————, take thee, —————————, to my wedded husband, to have and to hold from this day forward, for better for worse, for richer for poorer, in sickness and in health, love, cherish, till death us do part, according to God's holy ordinance; and there to I give thee my troth.

Then shall they again loose their hands; and the man shall give unto the woman a ring on this wise; the minister taking the ring shall deliver it unto the man, to put it upon the third finger of the woman's left hand. And the man, holding the ring there, and taught by the minister, shall say:

With this ring I thee wed: in the Name of the Father, and of the Son, and of the Holy Ghost. Amen.

And before delivering the ring to the man, the minister may say as follows:

Bless, O Lord, this ring, that he who gives it and she who wears it may abide in thy peace, and continue in thy favour, unto their life's end; through Jesus Christ our Lord. Amen.

Then the man leaving the ring upon the third finger of the woman's left hand, the minister shall say:

Let us pray.

Then shall the minister and the people, still standing, say the Lord's Prayer,

Our Father, who art in heaven, hallowed be thy Name; Thy kingdom come; Thy will be done on earth, as it is in heaven; Give us this day our daily bread: And forgive us our trespasses, as we forgive those who trespass against us; And lead us not into temptation; But deliver us from evil; For thine is the kingdom, and the power and the glory, for ever and ever. Amen.

Then shall the minister add,

O eternal God, Creator and Preserver of all mankind, Giver of all spiritual grace, the Author of everlasting life; send thy blessing upon these thy servants, this man and this woman, whom we bless in thy Name; that they, living faithfully together, may surely perform and keep the vow and covenant between them made (whereof this ring given and received is a token and pledge), and may ever remain in perfect love and peace together, and live according to thy laws; through Jesus Christ our Lord. Amen.

The minister may add one or both of the following prayers

O almighty God, Creator of mankind, who only art the wellspring of life; bestow upon these thy servants, if it be thy will, the gift and heritage of children; and grant that they may see their children brought up in thy faith and fear, to the honour and glory of thy Name; through Jesus Christ our Lord. Amen.

O God, who hast so consecrated the state of matrimony that in it is represented the spiritual marriage and unity betwixt Christ and his church; Look mercifully upon these thy servants, that they may love, honour, and cherish each other, and so live together in faithfulness and patience, in wisdom and true godliness, that their home may be a haven of blessing and of peace; through the same Jesus Christ our Lord, who liveth and reigneth with thee and the Holy Spirit ever, one God, world without end. Amen.

Then shall the minister join their right hands together, and say,

Those whom God hath joined together, let no man put asunder.

Then shall the minister speak unto the company,

Forasmuch as ＿＿＿＿＿＿, and ＿＿＿＿＿＿, have consented together in holy wedlock, and have witnessed the same before God and this company, and thereto have given and pledged their troth, each to the other, and have declared the same by giving and receiving a ring, and by joining hands; I pronounce that they are man and wife, In the name of the Father, and of the Son, and of the Holy Ghost. Amen.

The man and wife kneeling, the minister shall add this blessing,

God the Father, God the Son, God the Holy Ghost,

bless, preserve, and keep you: the Lord mercifully with his favor look upon you, and fill you with all spiritual benediction and grace; that ye may so live together in this life, that in the world to come ye may have life everlasting. Amen.

The laws respecting Matrimony, whether by publishing the Banns, in Churches, or by license, being different in the several states, every minister is left to the direction of those laws, in every thing that regards the civil contract between the parties.

And when the Banns are published it shall be in the following form: I publish the Banns of Marriage between N._____ and N._____. If any of you know cause, or just impediment, why these two persons should not be joined together in holy matrimony, ye are to declare it. This is the first, (second, or third) time of asking.

Note: From the Book of Common Prayer, dated 1945, certified by the Rev. John Wallace Suter. Approved by the Reverend Canon Charles M. Guilbert, Custodian of the Standard Book of Common Prayer (1966).

CHAPTER 18

A LUTHERAN ORDER FOR MARRIAGE

Before solemnizing a marriage, the minister shall counsel with the persons about to be married, and shall diligently inquire; first, as to whether the union contemplated be in accordance with the Word of God; second, whether it be in accordance with the laws of the State. No marriage shall be solemnized unless the minister be convinced that God's blessing may properly be asked upon it.

The minister may publish the Banns in the church, one or more Sundays, before the day appointed for the marriage, saying: N.N. and N.N. purpose to enter into the holy estate of matrimony, according to God's ordinance. They desire that prayer be made for them, that they may enter into this union in the name of the Lord, and be prospered in it. If any one can show just cause why they should not be joined together, I exhort him to make known such objection before the day of the marriage.

All arrangements for the marriage service shall be made in consultation with the pastor. Due reverence shall be maintained in the preparation for, and the celebration of, the marriage. The use of secular music shall not be permitted in the church.

When a marriage is solemnized in the church, a hymn may be sung, and Psalm 67 or Psalm 128 may be sung or said, ending with the Gloria Patri. If there be an address it may then follow.

The Congregation shall stand for the Invocation.

The persons to be married having presented themselves at the entrance to the chancel, or before the altar, the man to the right of the woman, the minister shall say:

In the Name of the Father, and of the Son, and of the Holy Ghost. Amen.

Dearly beloved; Forasmuch as Marriage is a holy estate, ordained of God, and to be held in honor by all, it becometh those who enter therein to weigh, with reverent minds, what the Word of God teacheth concerning it:

The Lord God said:

It is not good that the man should be alone; I will make him an helpmeet for him.

Our Lord Jesus Christ said:

Have ye not read that he which made them at the beginning, made them male and female, and said, For this cause shall a man leave father and mother, and shall cleave to his wife, and they twain shall be one flesh? Wherefore, they are no more twain, but one flesh. What therefore God hath joined together, let not man put asunder.

Then shall he read one or both of the following Lections:

The Apostle Paul, speaking by the Holy Spirit, saith:

Husbands, love your wives, even as Christ also loved the church, and gave himself for it. He that loveth his wife, loveth himself; for no man ever yet hated his own flesh, but nourisheth it, even as the Lord the church. Wives, submit yourselves unto your own husbands, as unto the Lord; for the husband is the head of the wife, even as Christ is the Head of the church.

The Apostle Peter, speaking by the Holy Spirit, saith:

Ye wives, let your adorning be the ornament of a meek and quiet spirit, which is, in the sight of God, of great price. Likewise, ye husbands, dwell with them according to knowledge, giving honor unto the wife as unto the weaker vessel and as being heirs together of the grace of life.

Then shall the minister say:

And although, by reason of sin, many a cross hath been laid thereon, nevertheless our gracious Father in heaven doth not forsake his children in an estate so holy and acceptable to him, but is ever present with his abundant blessing.

If the Banns have not been published, then the minister may say:

Into this holy estate this man and this woman come now to be united. If any one, therefore, can show just cause why they may not be lawfully joined together, let him now speak, or else forever hold his peace.

Then shall the minister say to the man:

_____, wilt thou have this woman to thy wedded wife, to live together after God's ordinance in the holy estate of matrimony? Wilt thou love her, comfort her, honor and keep her in sickness and in health, and, forsaking all others, keep thee only unto her, so long as you both shall live?

The man shall say:

I will.

Then the minister shall say to the woman:

_____, wilt thou have this man to thy wedded husband, to live together after God's ordinance in the holy estate of matrimony? Wilt thou love him, comfort him, honor and keep him in sickness and in health, and, forsaking all others, keep thee only unto him, so long as ye both shall live?

The woman shall say:

I will.

If the woman be given in marriage, the minister shall say:

Who giveth this woman to be married to this man?

The minister shall then receive her at the hands of her father (or guardian or any friend), the woman placing her right hand in the hand of the minister. Then shall the minister place the right hand of the woman in the right hand of the man. Then shall they loose their hands.

If the first part of the service has been conducted at the entrance to the chancel, the minister shall now precede the man and the woman to the altar.

The man shall take the right hand of the woman and say after the minister:

I, _____, take thee, _____, to my wedded wife, to have and to hold from this day forward, for better for worse, for richer for poorer, in sickness and in health, to love and to cherish, till death us do part, according to God's holy ordinance; and thereto I plight thee my troth.

Then shall the woman, in like manner, say after the minister:

I, _____, take thee, _____, to my wedded husband, to have and to hold from this day forward, for better for worse, for richer for poorer, in sickness and in health, to love and to cherish, till death us do part, according to God's holy ordinance; and thereto I plight thee my troth.

Should a shorter form be desired, the following may be said:

I, _____, take thee, _____, to my wedded wife (wife, or husband), and plight thee my troth, till death us do part.

If the wedding ring be used, the minister shall now receive it and give it to the man to put on the third finger of the woman's left hand.

Then shall the man say, or if two rings be used, the man and the woman, in turn, shall say, after the minister:

Receive this ring as a token of wedded love and troth.

Then shall the minister say:

Join your right hands.

Then shall the minister lay his right hand upon their hands and say:

Forasmuch as _____ and _____ have consented together in holy wedlock, and have declared the same before God and in the presence of this company, I pronounce them man and wife: In the Name of the Father and of the Son and of the Holy Ghost. Amen.

What God hath joined together, let not man put asunder.

Then may they kneel, and the minister shall bless them, saying:

The Lord God, who created our first parents and sanctified their union in marriage: Sanctify and bless you, that ye may please him both in body and soul, and live together in holy love until life's end. Amen.

Then shall the minister say:

Let us pray.

Almighty and most merciful God, Who hast now united this man and this woman in the holy estate of matrimony: Grant them grace to live therein according to Thy Holy Word; strengthen them in constant fidelity and true affection toward each other; sustain and defend them amidst all trials and temptations; and help them so to pass through this world in faith toward Thee, in communion with Thy Holy Church, and in loving service one of the other, that they may enjoy forever Thy heavenly benediction; through Jesus Christ, Thy Son, our Lord, Who liveth and reigneth with thee and the Holy Ghost, even one God, world without end. holy love until life's end. Amen.

The minister may add one or both of the following prayers:

O almighty God, Creator of mankind, who only art the well-spring of life: Bestow upon these thy servants, if it be thy will, the gift and heritage of children; and grant that they may see their children brought up in thy faith and fear, to the honor and glory of thy Name; through Jesus Christ our Lord. Amen.

O God, who art our dwelling-place in all generations: Look with favor upon the homes of our land; enfold husbands and wives, parents and children, in the bonds of thy pure love; and so bless our homes, that they may be a shelter for the defenseless, a bulwark for the tempted, a resting-place for the weary, and a foretaste of our eternal home in thee; through Jesus Christ our Lord. Amen.

Then shall all say:

Our Father . . . (the Lord's Prayer)

Then shall the minister say the Benediction:

The Lord bless thee and keep thee. The Lord make his

face shine upon thee, and be gracious unto thee. The Lord lift up his countenance upon thee, and give thee peace. Amen.

God almighty send you his light and truth to keep you all the days of your life. The hand of God protect you; his holy Angels accompany you. God the Father, God the Son, and God the Holy Ghost, cause his grace to be mighty upon you. Amen.

Note: From The Service Book and Hymnal of the Lutheran Church in the United States and Canada. Used by permission. Signed by The Reverend R. Seaman, S.T.D., Souderton, Pennsylvania.

CHAPTER 19

THE MARRIAGE SERVICE OF THE METHODIST CHURCH

At the time appointed, the persons to be married — having been qualified according to the law of the State and the standards of the church — standing together facing the Minister, the man at the Minister's left hand and the woman at the right, the Minister shall say:

Dearly beloved, we are gathered together here in the sight of God and in the presence of these witnesses, to join this man and this woman in holy matrimony, which is an honorable estate, instituted by God, and signifying unto us the mystical union which exists between Christ and his church; It is therefore not to be entered into unadvisedly, but reverently, discreetly, and in the fear of God. Into this holy estate these two persons come now to be joined.

Speaking to the persons to be married, the minister shall say:

I charge you both, as you stand in the presence of God, to remember that love and loyalty alone will avail as the foundation of a happy home. If the solemn vows which you are about to make be kept inviolate, and if steadfastly you endeavor to do the will of your Heavenly Father, your life will be full of joy, and the home which you are establishing will abide in peace. No other human ties are more tender, no other vows more sacred than those you now assume.

Then shall the minister say to the man, using his Christian name:

--------------------, wilt thou have this woman to be thy wedded wife, to live together in the holy estate of matrimony? Wilt thou love her, comfort her, honor and keep her, in sickness and in health; and forsaking all others keep thee only unto her, so long as ye both shall live?

The man shall answer:

I will.

Then shall the minister say to the woman using her Christian name:

——————————, wilt thou have this man to be thy wedded husband, to live together in the holy estate of matrimony? Wilt thou love him, honor and keep him, in sickness and in health; and forsaking all others keep thee only unto him, so long as ye both shall live?

The woman shall answer:

I will.

Then may the minister say:

Who giveth this woman to be married to this man?

The father of the woman, or whoever giveth her in marriage, shall answer:

I do.

Then the minister (receiving the hand of the woman from her father or other sponsor) shall cause the man with his right hand to take the woman by the right hand, and say after him:

I, ——————————, take thee, ——————————, to be my wedded wife, to have and to hold, from this day forward, for better, for worse, for richer, for poorer, in sickness and in health, to love and to cherish, till death us do part, and thereto I plight thee my faith.

Then shall they loose their hands; and the woman with her right hand taking the man by his right hand, shall likewise say after the minister:

I, ——————————, take thee, ——————————, to be my wedded husband, to have and to hold, from this day forward, for better, for worse, for richer, for poorer, in sickness and in health, to love and to cherish, till death us do part, and therefore I plight thee my faith.

Then shall they again loose their hands; and the man may give unto the woman a ring, on this wise; the minister taking the ring, shall say:

The wedding ring is the outward and visible sign of an inward and spiritual bond which unites two loyal hearts in endless love.

The minister shall then deliver the ring to the man to put upon the third finger of the woman's left hand. The man, holding the ring there, shall say after the minister:

In token and pledge of the vow between us made, with this ring I thee wed; in the name of the Father, and of the Son, and of the Holy Spirit. Amen.

In case of a double ring ceremony, the minister shall deliver the other ring to the woman, to put upon the third finger of the man's left hand, and the woman, holding the ring there, shall say after the minister:

In token and pledge of the vow between us made, with this ring I thee wed: in the name of the Father, and of the Son, and of the Holy Spirit. Amen.

Then shall the minister say:

Let us pray.

O eternal God, Creator and Preserver of all mankind, Giver of all spiritual grace, the Author of everlasting life, send thy blessing upon this man and this woman, whom we bless in thy Name; that they may surely perform and keep the vow and covenant now between them made.

Look graciously upon them, that they may love, honor and cherish each other, and so live together in faithfulness and patience, in wisdom and true godliness, that their home may be a haven of blessing and a place of peace; through Jesus Christ our Lord. Amen.

Then shall the minister join their right hands together and with his hand on their united hands shall say:

Forasmuch as _____, and _____, have consented together in holy wedlock, and have witnessed the same before God and this company, and thereto have pledged their faith each to the other, and have declared the same by joining hands, and by giving and receiving a ring; I pronounce that they are husband and wife together, in the Name of the Father, and of the Son, and of the Holy Spirit. Amen. Those whom God hath joined together, let no man put asunder. Amen.

Then the husband and wife kneeling, the minister shall say:

Let us pray.

Our Father . . . (The Lord's Prayer)

Then shall the minister add this blessing:

God the Father, the Son, and the Holy Spirit, bless, preserve, and keep you; the Lord graciously with his favor look upon you, and so fill you with all spiritual benediction and love that you may so live together in this life that in the world to come you may have life everlasting. Amen.

Note: The above marriage ceremony was copied from The Methodist Hymnal, 1939 edition. A minister may vary the wording if he desires, says Dr. Gaston Foote, Minister, First Methodist Church, Fort Worth, Texas.

CHAPTER 20

THE PRESBYTERIAN MARRIAGE CEREMONY

Forasmuch as marriage is a sacred relation, the ground of human fellowship and society, and most precious to mankind; although it be not a Sacrament nor peculiar to the Church of Christ, it is proper that it be solemnized by a lawful minister, that he may give counsel from the Word of God to those entering holy wedlock, and invoke the divine blessing upon them. — Directory for Worship, Chapter XII.

(The persons to be married shall present themselves before the minister, the woman standing at the left hand of the man. Then, all present reverently standing, the minister shall say to the company:)

Dearly beloved, we are assembled here in the presence of God, to join this man and this woman in holy marriage; which is instituted of God, regulated by His commandments, blessed by our Lord Jesus Christ, and to be held in honor among all men. Let us therefore reverently remember that God has established and sanctified marriage, for the welfare and happiness of mankind. Our Saviour has declared that a man shall leave his father and mother and cleave unto his wife. By His apostles, He has instructed those who enter into this relation to cherish a mutual esteem and love; to bear with each other's infirmities and weaknesses; to comfort each other in sickness, trouble, and sorrow; in honesty and industry to provide for each other, and for their household in temporal things; to pray for and encourage each other in the things which pertain to God; and to live together as heirs of the grace of life.

(Then speaking unto the persons who are to be married, he shall say:)

Forasmuch as you have come hither to be made one in this holy estate, I charge you both, that if either of you know any reason why you may not rightly be joined together in marriage, you do now acknowledge it. For be well assured that if any persons are joined together otherwise than as God's Word allows, their union is not blessed by Him.

(Then if no obstacle appears, the minister shall say:)

Let us pray.

Almighty and ever blessed God, whose presence is the happiness of every condition, and whose favor hallows every relation, we beseech Thee to be present and favourable unto these Thy servants, that they may be truly joined in the honourable estate of marriage, in the covenant of their God. As Thou hast brought them together by Thy providence, sanctify them by Thy Spirit, giving them a new frame of heart fit for their new estate; and enrich them with all grace, whereby they may enjoy the comforts, undergo the cares, endure the trials, and perform the duties of life together as becometh Christians, under Thy heavenly guidance and protection; through our Lord Jesus Christ. Amen.

(Then the minister shall say to the man,)

————————, wilt thou have this woman to be thy wife, and wilt thou pledge thy troth to her, in all love and honour, in all duty and service, in all faith and tenderness, to live with her, and cherish her, according to the ordinance of God, in the holy bond of marriage?

(The man shall answer,)

I will.

(Then the minister shall say to the woman,)

————————, wilt thou have this man to be thy husband, and wilt thou pledge thy troth to him, in all love and honour, in all duty and service, in all faith and tenderness, to live with him, and cherish him, according to the ordinance of God, in the holy bond of marriage?

(The woman shall answer,)

I will.

(Then the minister may say,)

Who giveth this woman to be married to this man?

(Then the father (or guardian or any friend) of the woman shall put her right hand into the right hand of the minister, who shall cause the man with his right hand to take her right hand and to say after him as follows:)

I, _____, take thee, _____, to be my wedded wife; and I do promise and covenant, before God and these witnesses, to be thy loving and faithful husband; in plenty and in want, in joy and in sorrow; in sickness and in health; as long as we both shall live.

(Then shall they loose their hands; and the woman with her right hand taking the man by his right hand, shall likewise say after the minister:)

I, _____, take thee, _____, to be my wedded husband; and I do promise and covenant, before God and these witnesses, to be thy loving and faithful wife, in plenty and in want, in joy and in sorrow; in sickness and in health; as long as we both shall live.

(Then, if a ring is provided, it shall be given to the minister, who shall return it to the man, who then shall put it upon the third finger of the woman's left hand, saying after the minister:)

This ring I give thee, in token and pledge, of our constant faith, and abiding love.

(Then the minister shall say:)

Let us pray.

Most merciful and gracious God, of whom the whole family in heaven and earth is named, bestow upon these Thy servants the seal of Thine approval, and Thy fatherly benediction; granting unto them grace to fulfil, with pure and steadfast affection, the vow and covenant between them made. Guide them together, we beseech Thee, in the way of righteousness and peace, that, loving and serving Thee, with one heart and mind, all the days of their life, they may be abundantly enriched with the tokens of Thine everlasting favour, in Jesus Christ our Lord. Amen.

Our Father, who art in heaven, hallowed be Thy Name; Thy kingdom come; Thy will be done on earth, as it is in heaven; Give us this day our daily bread: And forgive us our debts, as we forgive our debtors; And lead us not into temptation; But deliver us from evil; For Thine is the kingdom, and the power, and the glory, for ever. Amen.

(Then shall the minister say unto all who are present:)

By the authority committed unto me as a Minister of the Church of Christ, I declare that _____ and _____ are now husband and wife, according to the ordinance of God, and the law of the State; in the name of the Father, and of the Son, and of the Holy Spirit. Amen.

(Then causing the husband and wife to join their right hands, the minister shall say:)

Whom therefore God hath joined together, let no man put asunder.

(And the minister shall pronounce the Benediction:)

The Lord bless you, and keep you;
    The Lord make his face to shine upon you, and
        be gracious unto you;
    The Lord lift up His countenance upon you,
        and give you peace,
Both now and in the life everlasting. Amen.

Note: From *The Book of Common Worship,* copyright 1946 by the Board of Christian Education of the Presbyterian Church U.S.A. Used by permission.

CHAPTER 21

THE CATHOLIC MARRIAGE CEREMONY

THE MASS ON THE DAY OF MARRIAGE

(Couples married without a Mass may obtain the nuptial blessing any time after marriage, e.g., on the occasion of a wedding anniversary.)

INSTRUCTIONS BEFORE MARRIAGE

Dear friends in Christ: as you know, you are about to enter into a union which is most sacred and most serious, most sacred because established by God Himself, most serious because it will bind you together for life in a relationship so close and so intimate that it will profoundly influence your whole future. That future, with its hopes and disappointments, its successes and its failures, its pleasures and its pain, its joys and its sorrows, is hidden from your eyes. You know that these elements are mingled in every life, and are to be expected in your own. And so, not knowing what is before you, you take each other for better or for worse, for richer or for poorer, in sickness and in health, until death.

Truly, then, these words are most serious. It is a beautiful tribute to your undoubted faith in each other, that recognizing their full import, you are nevertheless so willing and ready to pronounce them. And because these words involve such solemn obligations, it is most fitting that you rest the security of your wedded life upon the great principle of self-sacrifice. And so you begin your married life by the voluntary and complete surrender of your individual lives in the interest of that deeper and wider life which you are to have in common. Henceforth you belong entirely to each other; you will be one in mind, one in heart, and one in affection. And whatever sacrifices you will be required to make to preserve this common life, always make them generously. Sacrifice is usually difficult and irksome. Only love can make it easy; and perfect love can make it a joy. We are willing to give in proportion as we love. And when love is perfect, the sacrifice is complete. God so loved the world that He gave His only begotten Son; and the Son so loved that He gave Himself for our salvation. "Greater love than this no man hath, that a man lay down his life for His friends."

No greater blessing can come to your married life, than that pure, conjugal love, loyal and true to the end. May, then, this love with which you join your hands and hearts today, never fail, but grow deeper and stronger as the years go on. And if true love and the unselfish spirit of perfect sacrifice guide your every action, you can expect the greatest measure of earthly happiness that may be allotted to man in this vale of tears. The rest is in the hands of God. Nor will God be wanting to your needs; He will pledge the lifelong support of His graces in the Holy Sacrament which you are now going to receive.

THE MARRIAGE CEREMONY

The Priest asks the Bridegroom (standing)

M _____, will you take W _____, here present, for your lawful wife according to the rite of our holy Mother, the Church?

Response:

I will.

Then the Priest asks the Bride:

M _____, will you take W _____, here present, for your lawful husband according to the rite of our holy Mother, the Church?

Response:

I will.

The consent of one is not sufficient; it must be expressed in some sensible sign by both. After obtaining their consent, the Priest bids the man and the woman join their right hands.

The man says after the Priest:

I, M _____, take you, W _____, for my lawful wedded wife, to have and to hold, from this day forward, for better, for worse, for richer, for poorer, in sickness and in health, until death do us part.

Then the woman says after the Priest:

I, W _____, take you, M _____, for my lawful husband, to have and to hold, from this day forward, for better, for worse, for richer, for poorer, in sickness and in health, until death do us part.

The Bridegroom and the Bride may kneel, and the Priest says:

I join you together in marriage in the name of the Father, and of the Son, and of the Holy Spirit. Amen.

He then sprinkles them with holy water. This done, the Priest blesses the ring(s) saying:

Versicle: Our help is in the name of the Lord.

Response: Who made heaven and earth.

V., O Lord, hear my prayer.

R., And let my cry come unto Thee.

V., The Lord be with you.

R., And with your spirit.

Let us pray: Bless, O Lord, this ring, which we bless in Thy Name, so that she who is to wear it, keeping true faith with her husband, may abide in Thy peace and obedience to Thy will, and ever live in mutual love. Through Christ our Lord.

R., Amen.

The Priest sprinkles the ring(s).

The Groom having received the ring from the hand of the Priest, puts it on the third finger of the left hand of the Bride and repeats after the Priest: "With this ring I thee wed, and plight unto thee my troth."

The Priest then says:

In the name of the Father, and of the Son, and of the Holy Ghost.

Confirm, O God, this work which you have begun in us, from your holy temple, which is in Jerusalem.

V., Lord, have mercy.

R., Christ, have mercy,

Our Father, (silently).

V., And lead us not into temptation.

R., But deliver us from evil.

V., Grant salvation to Thy servants.

R., For their hope, O my God, is in Thee.

V., Send them aid, O Lord, from Thy holy place.

R., And watch over them from Sion.

V., O Lord, hear my prayer.

R., And let my cry come unto Thee.

V., The Lord be with you.

R., And with your spirit.

Let us pray. Look down, we beseech Thee, O Lord, upon these Thy servants and graciously protect Thy institutions, whereby Thou hast provided for the propagation of mankind; that those who are joined together by Thine authority may be preserved by Thy help. Through Christ our Lord. Amen.

The Mass follows:

After the "Our Father" the Priest interrupts the usual sequence of the Mass, and turning to the bridal couple who kneel before the altar, confers the Nuptial Blessing upon them.

Let us pray. Listen with favor, O Lord, to our prayers, and in Thy goodness maintain the ways which Thou hast established for the continuation of the human race, so that the union which has been founded by Thy authority may be preserved by Thy aid. Through our Lord Jesus Christ, Thy Son, Who lives and reigns with Thee in the unity of the Holy Spirit, God, world without end.

R., Amen.

Let us pray, O God, who by Thy mighty power hast made all things where before there was nothing; Who having put in order the beginnings of the universe, didst form for man, made to Thy image, an inseparable helpmate, woman, so that Thou didst give woman's body its origin from man's flesh, and teach that it is never right to separate her from the one being whence it has pleased Thee to take her;

O God, Who hast consecrated the union of marriage making it a sign so profound as to prefigure in the marriage covenant the mystery of Christ and the Church:

O God, Who dost join woman to man, and give to that society, the first to be established, the blessing which alone was not taken away in punishment for original sin nor in the doom of the Flood;

Look with kindness on this Thy servant, who is now to be joined to her husband in the companionship of marriage and who seeks to be made secure by Thy protection.

May this yoke that she is taking on herself be one of love and peace. May she be faithful and chaste, marrying in Christ and may she always imitate the holy women. May she be the beloved of her husband, as was Rachel; wise, as was Rebecca, longlived and loyal, as was Sarah.

May the author of sin have no mastery over her because of her acts. May she hold firm to the Faith, and commandments. Faithful to one embrace, may she flee from unlawful companionship. By firm discipline may she fortify herself against her weakness. May she be grave in her modesty, honorable in her chastity, learned in the teachings of heaven.

May she be rich in children, prove worthy and blameless, and may she attain in the end to the peace of the blessed, the Kingdom of heaven.

May she and her husband together see their children's children to the third and fourth generation and enjoy the long life they desire. Through our Lord Jesus Christ Thy Son, who lives and reigns with Thee in the unity of the Holy Spirit, God, for ever and ever.

R., Amen.

Before the last blessing of the Mass, the Priest once more turns to the bridal couple and gives the final blessing of the Church, after which he sprinkles them with holy water.

May the God of Abraham, the God of Isaac, the God of Jacob be with you, and may He fulfill in you His blessing; so that you may see your children's children to the third and fourth generation and afterwards possess everlasting and boundless life. Through the help of our Lord Jesus Christ, Who with the Father and the Holy Spirit lives and reigns God, forever and ever. Amen.

Note: This marriage ceremony was taken from "The Catholic Marriage Manual" by the Rev. George A. Kelly. Published by Random House, Inc., 1958. Permission granted.

Selection:

Specified excerpt (pp. 210-213) from the Catholic Marriage Manual, by Msgr. George A. Kelley.

Acknowledgment:

From the Catholic Marriage Manual, by Msgr. George A. Kelly. Copyright 1958 by Random House, Inc., reprinted by permission.

CHAPTER 22

A JEWISH MARRIAGE SERVICE

Blessed be he that cometh in the name of the Lord; (we bless you out of the house of the Lord.)

Serve the Lord with gladness; come before Him with singing.

O God supremely blessed, supreme in might and glory, guide and bless this bridegroom and bride.

Unto Thee, O God and Father, we lift our souls in praise. All creation declares Thy glory; through man, fashioned in Thine image, Thou hast revealed Thy majesty. Within his heart Thou hast implanted the ennobling influences of love and devotion. Thou Who art the Source of life and of joy, bless the covenant which this bridegroom and bride now seal in Thy name. Be with them in this sacred hour and in all the days to come. Amen.

MARRIAGE SERVICES

Address by Rabbi may be delivered here.
(To the bridegroom):

Do you _____ take _____ to be your wife, promising to cherish and protect her, whether in good fortune or in adversity, and to seek together with her a life hallowed by the faith of Israel?

(To the bride):

Do you _____ take _____ to be your husband, promising to cherish and protect him, whether in good fortune or in adversity, and to seek together with him a life hallowed by the faith of Israel?

Benedictions:

Blessed art Thou, O Lord our God, Ruler of the Universe, Who hast created all things for Thy glory.

Blessed art Thou, O Lord our God, Ruler of the Universe, Creator of man.

Blessed art Thou, O Lord our God, Ruler of the Universe, Who hast fashioned us in Thine own image and hast established marriage for the fulfillment and perpetuation of life in accordance with Thy holy purpose. Blessed art Thou, O Lord, Creator of man.

Blessed art Thou, O Lord our God, Ruler of the Universe, Who art the source of all gladness and joy. Through Thy grace we attain affection, companionship, and peace. Grant, O Lord, that the love which unites this bridegroom and bride may grow in abiding happiness. May their family life be ennobled through their devotion to the faith of Israel. May there be peace in their home, quietness and confidence in their hearts. May they be sustained by Thy comforting presence in the midst of our people and by Thy promise of salvation for all mankind. Blessed art Thou, O Lord, Who dost unite bridegroom and bride in holy joy. Amen.

Blessed art Thou, O Lord our God, Ruler of the Universe, Creator of the fruit of the vine.

(The wine is offered to the bridegroom and bride.)

As you have shared the wine from this cup, so may you, under God's guidance, draw contentment, comfort and felicity from the cup of life. May you find life's joys heightened, its bitterness sweetened, and all things hallowed by true companionship and love.

(To the bridegroom) :

As you _____ place this ring upon the finger of your bride, speak to her these words:

With this ring be thou consecrated unto me as my wife according to the law of God and the faith of Israel.

(To the bride):

And you ＿＿＿＿ (place this ring upon your bridegroom's finger as a token of wedlock and) say unto him these words:

(With this ring) be thou consecrated unto me as my husband according to the law of God and the faith of Israel.

(Rabbi continues):

Blessed art Thou, O God, who sanctifiest Thy people Israel by the covenant of marriage.

In the presence of this company as witness you have spoken the words and performed the rites which unite your lives. I, therefore, declare you ＿＿＿＿ and ＿＿＿＿, husband and wife, married in accordance with the laws of the State of ＿＿＿＿ and according to the tradition of our Jewish faith.

And now I ask you and all your dear ones to bow your heads in reverence. Silently let us pray that God will bless your home and help you to achieve your highest hopes.

Pause for silent prayer.

May the Lord bless thee and keep thee.

May the Lord cause His countenance to shine upon thee and be gracious unto thee.

May the Lord lift up His countenance unto thee and give thee peace. Amen.

Note: Permission granted by Central Conference of American Rabbis, New York, N.Y., Rabbi Sidney L. Regner, Executive Vice President.

A CLASSIFIED BIBLIOGRAPHY ON MARRIAGE

For The Minister

Bailey, Derrick S. *The Mystery of Love and Marriage.* New York: Harper and Brothers, 1952.

Brav, Stanley R. (Editor). *Marriage and the Jewish Tradition.* New York: Philosophical Library.

Christensen, James L. *The Minister's Service Manual.* Westwood, New Jersey: Fleming H. Revell, 1960.

Dicks, Russell L. *Pastoral Work and Pastoral Counseling.* New York: The Macmillan Company.

Easton, Burton Scott and Robbing, Howard Chandler. *The Bond of Honour.* New York: The Macmillan Company.

Folkman, Rabbi Jerome D. *The Cup of Life.* New York: The Jonathan David Company.

Goodman, Philip and Hanna. *The Jewish Marriage Anthology.* Philadelphia: The Jewish Publication Society of America, 1965.

Hedley, George R. *The Minister Behind the Scenes.* New York: The Macmillan Company, 1956.

Hiltner, Seward. *Sex and the Christian Life.* New York: Association Press, 1957.

Hutton, S. W. *Minister's Service Manual.* Grand Rapids, Michigan: Baker Book House, 1964.

In Holy Matrimony. Nashville: The Methodist Publishing House, 1958.

Kemp, Charles F. *Physicians of the Soul, A History of Pastoral Counseling.* New York: The Macmillan Company, 1947.

Kuchler, Frances W. *Law of Engagement and Marriage.* New York: Oceana Publications, Inc.

Leach, William H. *The Cokesbury Marriage Manual.* Nashville: Abingdon Press, 1959.

May, Rollo. *The Art of Counseling.* Nashville: Abingdon Press, 1958.

Pike, James A. *If You Marry Outside Your Faith.* New York: Harper and Brothers, 1954.

Stewart, Charles William. *The Minister as Marriage Counselor.* Nashville: Abingdon Press, 1961.

The Pastor's Manual for Premarital Counseling. Nashville: The Methodist Publishing House, 1958.

Wood, Leland Foster and Dickinson, R. L. *Harmony in Marriage.* New York: Round Table Press, 1939.

FOR PARENTS

Bossard, James H. S. *Parent and Child.* Philadelphia: University of Pennsylvania Press, 1953.

Brown, Alberta Z. *Teens to Twenty-One.* St. Louis: Bethany Press, 1957.

Groves, Ernest R. *Conserving Marriage and the Family.* New York: The Macmillan Company, 1944.

Jones, Mary Alice. *Guiding Children in Christian Growth.* Nashville: Abingdon Press, 1949.

Kemp, Charles F. *Christian Dimensions of Family Living.* St. Louis: Bethany Press, 1964.

Kuchler, Frances W. H. *Law of Marriage and Divorce.* New York: Oceana Publications, 1959.

Mackay, Richard V. *Marriage and Divorce.* New York: Oceana Publications.

McKim, Judson J. *The Formal Wedding.* Westwood, New Jersey: Fleming H. Revell, 1947.

Parkhurst, Helen. *Exploring the Child's World.* New York: Appleton, Century, Croft, Inc., 1951.

Wynn, John Charles. *How Christian Parents Face Family Problems.* Philadelphia: The Westminster Press, 1955.

A Special Note—

A very timely study and work manual to be used by marriage counselors, ministers, teachers and couples preparing for marriage entitled *Grounds for Marriage,* by James R. Hine, McKinley Foundation, Champaign, Illinois, is available. In brief the contents include:

I. What you bring to your marriage
II. Adventure into mutuality
III. Personality traits compared
IV. The marriage union
V. Financing the home and the future
VI. Religious homes are happy homes
VII. Bibliography
VIII. Information sheets

PUBLICATIONS ON MARRIAGE AND PREPARATION FOR MARRIAGE

(1) "Christian Marriage" _____$ .10
General interpretation and practical suggestions of what makes a marriage Christian.

(2) "Harmony in Marriage" _____ 1.25
Harmonizing of personalities, physical harmony, parenthood, the spiritual meaning of family life.

(3) "If I Marry a Roman Catholic" _____ .05
Indicates the problems which must be faced when a Protestant marries a RC.

(4) "Marriage Troubles Can Be Overcome" _____ .05
Questions and discussion of the common reasons for marriage failure.

(5) "If I Marry Outside My Religion" _____ .25
The problems and obstacles faced by an interfaith marriage, some vital suggestions for meeting the difficulties.

(6) "Sex, Love, and Marriage" _____ .15
Informal, friendly interpretation of love; the place of sex; some criteria for judging one's maturity and readiness for marriage; the place of the church in the confusing problem.

(7) "Your First Week Together" _____ .10
A plan for devotions at the beginning of marriage. Carefully selected poems, Bible readings, prayers.

(8) "The Formal Wedding" _____ 1.50
By Judson J. McKim; introduction by Mrs. Charles P. Taft.

_____

(Note: The list above calls attention to only a few of the many pamphlets and books now available. Write either of these agencies.)

(Available through The Bethany Press, Box 179, St. Louis, or The National Council of the Churches of Christ in the United States of America, 475 Riverside Drive, New York City, New York 10027).

Date	Names	Places and Witnesses	The Continuing Ministry

Note: A minister may set up his own record system in line with
s training and experience. Initiative in this matter is suggested.

THE MINISTER'S RECORD OF MARRIAGES

Date	Names	Places and Witnesses	The Continuing Minis

Note: A minister may set up his own record system in line with his training and experience. Initiative in this matter is suggested.